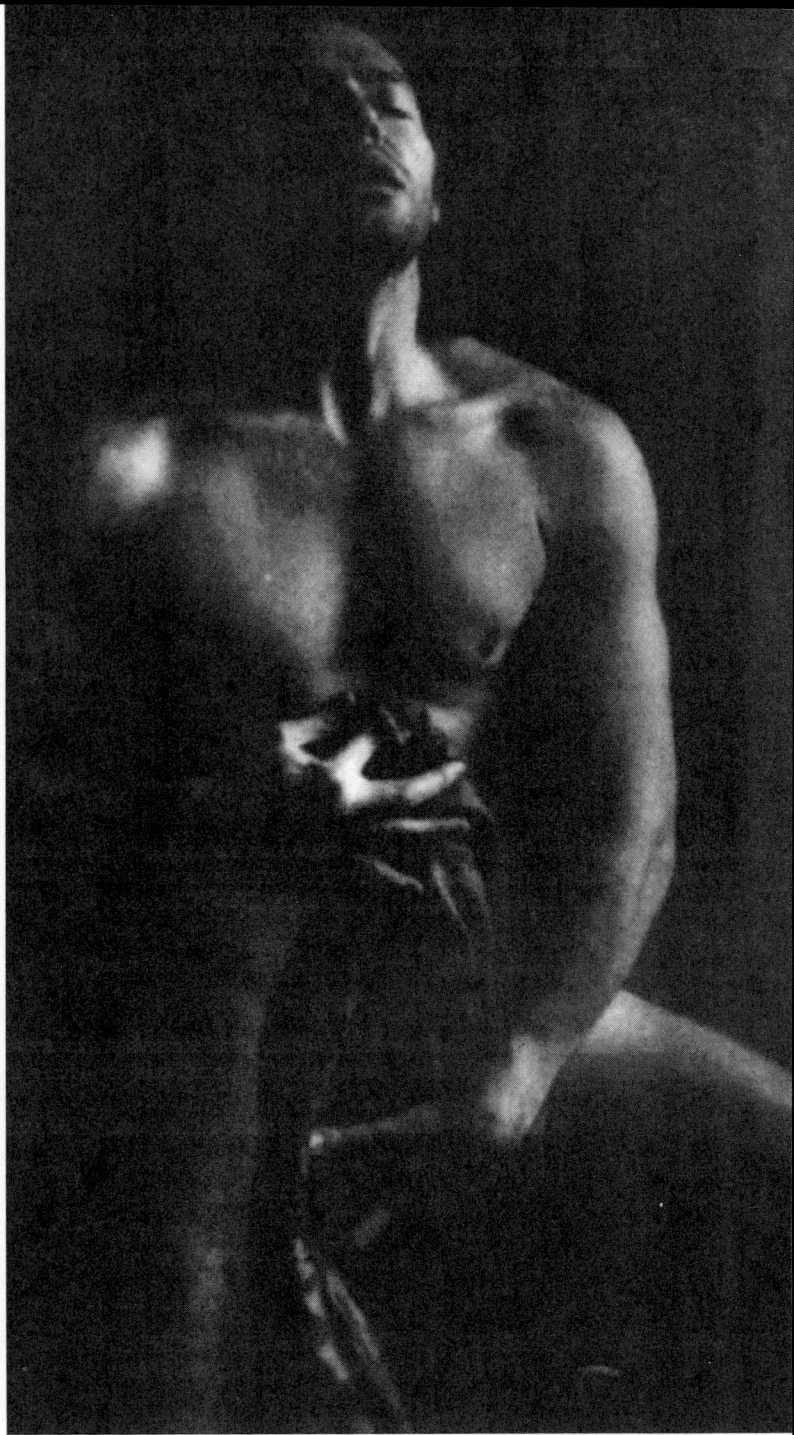

Danceland

Danceland

Glen Cairns

Playwrights Canada Press
Toronto • Canada

Playwrights Canada Press
54 Wolseley St., 2nd fl. Toronto, Ontario CANADA M5T 1A5
416-703-0013   fax 416-703-0059
orders@playwrightscanada.com • www.playwrightscanada.com

Playwrights Canada Press acknowledges the support of
the taxpayers of Canada and the province of Ontario through
The Canada Council for the Arts and the Ontario Arts Council.

The Canada Council for the Arts
Le Conseil des Arts du Canada

ONTARIO ARTS COUNCIL
CONSEIL DES ARTS DE L'ONTARIO

Cover photo of Kevin Howarth by Mark Douet.
Production Editor: Jodi Armstrong

National Library of Canada Cataloguing in Publication Data

Cairns, Glen
    Danceland / Glen Cairns.

A play.
ISBN 0-88754-637-4

    I. Title.

PS8555.A4622D35 2002   C812'.54   C2002-900090-4
PR9199.3.C257D35 2002

First edition: July 2002.
Printed and bound by AGMV Marquis at Quebec, Canada.

For T.K.
Who insisted that this is a love story.

ACKNOWLEDGEMENTS

Danceland could not have been completed without the invaluable support of The Canada Council for the Arts and the developmental assistance of The Saskatchewan Playwright's Centre, The Playwright's Theatre Centre of British Columbia, Touchstone Theatre, Vancouver, Crow's Theatre, Toronto, and Red River Productions in association with The Canadian High Commission in London, England.

HISTORICAL NOTE

As you drive through the potash belt of south central Saskatchewan, with the sun so low on the horizon at dawn and dusk that you seem to be chasing your own shadow, you reach a fissure in the earth's crust and plunge down, down, down to where a small remnant of an ancient salt sea breaks through the barren landscape in a fourteen kilometer long crescent of iridescent silver. This is Little Lake Manitou. On its far shore sits Danceland, stranded, but still glimmering white on a pier under which the water has long-since receded. Thorns and brush and beach grass grow below the dance hall which once seemed to float in the salt water at the edge of the lake.

When I first encountered this sight, I thought, "what the hell is that thing doing out here in the middle of nowhere?" Eighteen months in the local history rooms of the public libraries in Saskatoon and Watrous, answered that question. Built in the same year by the same company which built The Roseland Ballroom in Manhattan and The Commodore Ballroom in Vancouver, Danceland was the largest of the three, it's 4,800 square foot dancefloor built to float on a cushion of horse hair. It was commissioned by an enterprising local farmer who had been approached by The CPR with an offer to buy his lakefront land so that they could build a resort on the shores of the legendary "lake of healing waters." The apocryphal story goes that the farmer, being a cagey Scot, thought to himself, "well, if it's so special that the CPR wants to spend all that money, why don't I just do it myself?" He turned the offer down, and, in 1915, opened his own resort, complete with a state of the art dance hall.

By the mid 1920s his neighbours had emulated him and, with rail links direct to Chicago and Denver, Little Manitou had grown into a thriving resort destination with five dance halls, ten silent movie screens, a plethora of spas and, of course, hotels and bars serving legal Canadian whiskey to thirsty, Prohibition-era American tourists. History, it turns out, follows a perverse kind of accidental logic. Yet the place still haunted me. Jazz? In Saskatchewan in the 1920s and '30s? Bootlegging and booze in the heart of The Bible Belt? Urban American gangsters like Al Capone and John Dillinger in placid, small-town Canada? A decadent, roaring twenties vacation destination atop a sacred Native place of healing? The cultural contradictions were both startling and fascinating. So I began to write...

—Glen Cairns

This version of *Danceland* premiered at The Old Red Lion, London, England, November, 1995, produced by Red River Productions in association with The Canadian High Commission, with the following cast and crew:

LILY   DeNica Fairman
LLOYD   Peter Marinker
MURRAY   Kevin Howarth
ROSE   Catherine Holman

Directed by Tom Kerr
Set and Costumes designed by Lisa Robinson
Lighting designed by Lizz Poulter
Music Composed by The Brother Jonathan
Production/Stage Managed by Helen Dolan

Danceland evolved over a period of about five years and four productions. The first, seventy-five-minute version was produced by The Acme Explosives Co., Halifax, directed by Bryden Macdonald. The first ninety-minute version was produced by Fend Players at The Station Street Arts Centre, Vancouver, directed by Paul Crepeau. A significantly altered version of that text was produced by Crow's Theatre, Toronto, directed by Jim Millan. This, final version, was produced by Red River Productions, at The Old Red Lion, London, directed by Tom Kerr.

CHARACTERS

LILY   Stylish. Thirty-three. A singer.
LLOYD   Her husband. Mid-fifties. An American bandleader and clarinetist. Alcoholic. Lloyd has of late been confined to a wheelchair. He has been unable to work as a musician for some time.
MURRAY   Late twenties. Handsome. He owns and operates the boat taxi service on Little Manitou Lake.
ROSE   Murray's daughter. Pubescent.

TIME AND PLACE

Late August, 1934.
Little Manitou Beach, Saskatchewan.

SET

Should be as simple as possible. Evocative, not representative. Light and sound are the most pervasive scenic elements.

SOUND

The actor playing Lloyd need not play clarinet, although a familiarity with the embouchure and fingering patterns is helpful. The play benefits from musical underscoring with solo clarinet. The songs, however, should be sung *a cappella*. They are more like prayers or invocations; a continuation of the action of the scenes rather than musical "numbers."

NOTE: The name of the town, Bienfait, is pronounced "Bean-fay."

ACT ONE

— — *Scene One* — —

> *LLOYD's cabin. Brown's Sanatorium.*
>
> *Saturday. Dusk.*
>
> *LLOYD is sitting in his wheelchair, leafing through a worn volume of American poetry. He is excited. His hands tremble as he searches through the pages.*
>
> *LILY is changing out of beachwear, getting ready to go down to the dancehall for the night's gig.*

LLOYD (*finds the poem he's been looking for*) Here, here, here, here, here. Here it is, I found it. Ezra Pound, "The River Merchant's Wife." C'mere; siddown... I want to read this to you.

LILY Just hold your horses. Jeez, I'm going to be late. I knew I didn't have time to come down here for a swim; I should just have met you at Danceland after the gig.

LLOYD (*gentle*) Come on. Siddown. Just sit down and close your eyes for a minute. This is beautiful.

> *LILY slams a chair down and then sits on it.*
>
> *He reaches over and strokes her hair.*

LLOYD Listen. Just close your eyes and listen. It's the most beautiful thing in the world. This woman, this Chinese woman is talking...

LILY I've heard it before.

LLOYD ...I think it's supposed to be his girlfriend, Hilda. She was only about sixteen.

LILY Oh, the nasty man.

LLOYD	It's how she felt about Pound.
LILY	Are you sure it isn't how he felt about himself?
LLOYD	Don't be a cynic. She'd do anything for him; probably die.
LILY	*(dry)* Lucky him. *(beat)* Read me a different one, okay?
LLOYD	Alright. Here. I love this one, it's another Pound, it's called "Alba"; it's like a photograph. It's so beautiful, the way he describes her, just lying beside him, as cool as the wet leaves of Lily of the Valley.
LILY	But do they actually *do* anything, or does she just keep lying there like a plant?
LLOYD	Of course.
LILY	Does it say?
LLOYD	It's implied.
LILY	What's implied?
LLOYD	That they… you know.
LILY	What? Cross pollinate?

She purses her lips together and pretends to blow some dandelion down at him.

You're a hopeless romantic, Lloyd. You should get your mind out of books and back down in the gutter where it belongs.

She gets up and resumes dressing.

LILY	Who else is in there? Anybody a little more, oh, stimulating?

LLOYD	*(leafing through)* Sure. Lots of people. Emerson. Thoreau. Some Sandburg. I like Sandburg; met him in a bar in Chicago a couple of years back.
LILY	What's he like?
LLOYD	Sandburg? He's great, a great guy. He accompanies himself on guitar when he reads; he's pretty good, too. Musical but muscular; he writes real muscular verse.
LILY	Oh, I like that.
LLOYD	*(moving on)* Here's a couple by Emily Dickenson.
LILY	That morbid bitch.
LLOYD	Lily!
LILY	Well, she is. All those tombstones; death riding past in a horse-drawn carriage.
LLOYD	She was melancholy, that's all.
LILY	She was crazy. Did you ever meet her?
LLOYD	No. She died the year I was born.
LILY	Lucky you.
	They laugh.
LLOYD	Here. Here's some Whitman; Walt Whitman. "Give Me The Splendid Silent Sun." Does that sound good? Whaddaya think?
LILY	Whatever you want.
LLOYD	I love you all to pieces.
	LILY laughs and resumes dressing.
	LLOYD picks up a bottle of whisky off the floor beside him and takes a pull off it.

Then he begins to read.

"Give me the splendid silent sun with all his beams
full-dazzling
Give me autumnal fruit ripe and red from the
orchard,
Give me a field where the unmow'd grass grows,
Give me an arbor, give me the trellis'd grape, Give
me fresh corn and wheat, give me serene moving
animals teaching content,
Give me nights perfectly quiet as on high plateaus
west of the Mississippi, and I looking up at the
stars."

*He looks up at LILY for a moment, then continues
reading...*

LLOYD   "Give me odorous at sunrise a garden full of flowers where I can walk undisturbed,
Give me for marriage a sweet breath'd woman of
whom I should never tire,
Give me a perfect child, give me..."

He stops reading. His face is streaked with tears

LILY   God, I love you.

He closes the book and puts it down.

LLOYD   *(gruff)* Sorry. I forgot how maudlin the old pederast
could be. *(beat)* How was your swim?

LILY   Invigorating. You should try it.

LLOYD   Are you kidding? It's a goddamned swamp.

LILY   Little Manitou's a place of healing, Lloyd. People
have been coming here for years; the Assiniboines,
the Cree.

LLOYD   It's a smelly, sulphurous, evil goddamned swamp.
The water stinks and the sand is full of fleas, the
grass is full of ticks and the air is full of mosquitoes
the size of goddamned roosters! You couldn't get

the clap cured in a place like this. *(beat)* Nope. I'm a
city guy. Gimme the streets of Manhattan; give me
Detroit, Philadelphia; give me nightclubs and
Ellington; Satchmo. Give me Kansas City at dawn.
Give me New Orleans, with me and the band and
you up front, howling the blues like a wounded
she-wolf, standing all alone on the jagged edge of
the Atlantic City shore. *(beat)* I should have stayed
in Chicago and played with the band.

LILY   You couldn't have played with the band.

LLOYD   I could!

               Silence.

LLOYD   I'm a musician, Lily. I need to play. *(beat)*
Howzabout it? Tonight. Just one set.

LILY   Not without a rehearsal, Lloyd. Your style's too
strong; you'll throw my band offstride.

LLOYD   So fire the bums; we'll swing that dancehall single-
handed. Whaddaya say?

LILY   It's not that simple, I can't just…. *(beat)* Let's give
it another week, hunh? I don't want you to push
yourself too hard.

LLOYD   You afraid I'll embarrass you?

LILY   We've had a great day, Lloyd. Please don't start.

LLOYD   I'm not starting anything.

               Pause.

               LILY moves away to retrieve some clothing.

        I do embarrass you, don't I?

LILY   I'm going to pretend I didn't hear that, okay?

               She starts to pull a loose sundress over her head.

LLOYD	Where'd you get that mark?

> *LILY stops, mid-motion, to look down at her hip. LLOYD wheels over and puts his hand on her. LILY playfully slaps his hand away.*

LILY	You had all afternoon for that; you missed your chance.

> *LLOYD grabs at her.*

LLOYD	What is it? A love bite?
LILY	Around here? It's more like a flea bite, and you know it.

> *LLOYD grabs hold of her hand and won't let go.*

LLOYD	What's that supposed to mean?
LILY	Nothing. Just a joke.
LLOYD	You disappear up the beach for hours at a time. I don't know what you're doing, or who you're with...
LILY	Lloyd, we discussed this before we left Chicago...
LLOYD	...and how come you have to stay in some fancy hotel up in town...
LILY	...Lloyd... quit kidding around...
LLOYD	...when I'm stuck way the hell and gone out here?
LILY	...that's not funny.... Let go!

> *She breaks free.*
>
> *Pause.*

LLOYD	If I so much as smell him on you...

LILY   What are you…? Dillinger's dead, Lloyd. Some woman saw him coming out of a movie theatre in Chicago last month, the Cops set up an ambush and shot him down. *(beat)* I'd better go, I'm going to be late for work.

She scoops up the last of her things and heads for the door .

LLOYD   Wait a minute! Wait a minute… where are you… don't you walk out on me! I came twelve hundred miles to this goddamned swamp so that I could be with you…

LILY   Then BE with me! BE WITH ME!

Pause.

I love you, Lloyd. Believe me.

She moves in to him and wraps her arms around his chest, her face close to his ear.

You're my best one; my only one. *(beat)* Tell you what; I'll move my things out here from the hotel tomorrow. I can always keep the room at The Hiawatha for a getaway between sets. People I knew as a kid keep coming backstage to gawk at me. Presbyterians. God. I mean, what do they think? I moved to Chicago and grew horns?

LLOYD   Maybe they just wanna look up your ass to see if your hat's on straight.

They laugh. Then LILY moves around and sits, gently, on LLOYD's lap.

Careful. Careful.

LILY adjusts herself.

LILY   Better?

LLOYD I guess. I don't know.

LILY What? Should I get off?

She starts to get off him. He stops her.

LLOYD No, no. It's just... I don't know. *(beat)* Sometimes I feel like my bones are trying to crawl out through my skin. *(beat)* You're still so young.... *(beat)* Don't leave me, hunh? I couldn't bear it if you ever left me.

She leans in and kisses him, long and deep and hard. When they finish kissing, LILY gets up off LLOYD. She's crying. LLOYD reaches out and takes her hand.

It didn't hurt, you know. The gunshot. It just startled me more than anything; that first explosion. Then I was falling. I felt heat; waves of cramp in my belly. It all seemed to be happening so slow. *(beat)* I'll never forget the silence; the sight of those white hotel-room curtains hanging straight down; no breeze. Then far away, across the city, I heard the sirens start to wail. Police. Ambulance. *(beat)* Jazz everywhere. *(beat)* You were hovering over me like an angel. *(beat)* And I felt hate, Lily. I remember feeling hate... I'm a gentle man; but, hate... it feels hot; like a shot of whisky. *(beat)* I liked it, Lily. I liked the way hate felt.

He lets go of her hand.

Pause.

You'd better go, you're gonna' be late.

LILY They'll wait.

LLOYD They won't have much choice.

LLOYD picks the bottle off the floor and starts to wheel away.

LILY	Lloyd?

He stops, but doesn't look back.

LLOYD	Yeah?

Pause.

LILY	Save me a shot for later.

She turns to leave and almost trips over little ROSE, who has appeared in the doorway.

Jesus! Didn't anybody teach you to knock?

She takes a quick look back at LLOYD and then makes her way out the door.

ROSE just stands there, staring at LLOYD.

Pause.

LLOYD	So, what are you staring at?
ROSE	Nothin'.
LLOYD	Well, beat it then. Can't you see I'm busy?
ROSE	You're not busy; you were just fightin' with your wife.
LLOYD	I said, get lost.

He wheels away.

ROSE	Are you really a cripple?

LLOYD stops and turns back to her.

LLOYD	Look. Why don't you go home and tell your mother she wants you?
ROSE	Because she's dead.

LLOYD   Oh. Sorry.

                 Pause.

ROSE   If you're a cripple, how come I seen ya walkin' with
                 them stick things up the road to the east beach the
                 other day?

LLOYD   *(pointed)* What do you want? Just tell me and then
                 go away

ROSE   My Daddy's comin' by in the boat to pick me up
                 from visitin', and he told me special to come an' ask
                 ya's if ya wanted a ride up to Danceland for the
                 dancin' later on, seein' as how he's goin' up there
                 anyways an' he says it must be awful hard for
                 youse to get around.

LLOYD   Oh. *(beat)* No. No, thanks. Maybe later.

ROSE   He makes another run at nine, but it'll cost you a
                 quarter seein' as how it's a regular run an' not a
                 special like this time.

LLOYD   Well, I think I can afford it. I just don't want to go
                 yet.

                 *ROSE approaches him and puts her hand on his
                 knee.*

ROSE   Is it "arthuritis?"

LLOYD   *(sharp)* Don't be silly! *(beat)* It's not.... It's.... No, it's
                 not a disease.

ROSE   I just thought maybe it was "arthuritis." *(beat)* You'll
                 get better, though. Lotsa people do. They come here
                 an' swim in the lake an' then go home all better.
                 That's why Little Manitou's called The Lake Of
                 Healing Waters. All kindsa people come here all
                 sick an' cripply, an' then go home better.

LLOYD   *(considers)* Maybe they do. *(beat)* Maybe they do.

ROSE looks at him for a moment. Puzzled.

ROSE Don't be sad.

  She starts to crawl up onto his lap.

LLOYD Careful! Careful, careful, you might break my bones. **ROSE** I'm bein' as light an' careful as an angel.

LLOYD Easy. Easy. That's a girl.

  ROSE settles down on his lap and wraps her arms around him.

ROSE I'll be your angel for the summer if you want.

  MURRAY shouts from off, down at the pier.

MURRAY Rose! Where are ya? Rose?

ROSE I gotta' go. My Daddy's callin'.

  ROSE slips off LLOYD's lap and starts to go. Stops. Turns back to LLOYD.

ROSE Can I? Wouldja like that, if I was your angel for the summer?

MURRAY *(off)* Angel?! Rose?!

ROSE I could do stuff for ya?

LLOYD I don't know, sweetheart. You better go.

ROSE Please?

LLOYD Well…. *(beat)* Whatever you want.

  ROSE is elated.

ROSE Really? I can help you like an angel?

LLOYD   Sure. But the next time you come over, you knock.
               Understand?

ROSE   Oh, yes!

LLOYD   Now beat it.

               *She spins on her heels and heads out the door
               yelling at the top of her lungs...*

ROSE   Daddy! Daddy! I got somebody to help, just like an
               angel! I got somebody to help! I got somebody to
               help!

               *LLOYD watches her go. Smiles. Then wheels
               across the room.*

               *There is thunder, low and rumbling in the
               distance.*

               Fade out as.... A smoky jazz riff plays.

— — *Scene Two* — —

               *Fade in. The interior of Danceland, Early Sunday
               morning.*

               *Dawn is breaking through a single pane window.
               A dusty white curtain billows on a gentle breeze.*

               *LILY walks through the deserted dancehall, smok-
               ing a cigarette. Her silk dressing gown flows out
               behind her.*

               She sings quietly to herself.

               *The doors to Danceland swing open. Sunlight
               slashes into the space.*

               LILY is startled. She stops singing abruptly.

               *A man is standing in the doorway, framed by the
               light. LILY can't make out who he is.*

MURRAY   *(laconically)* Knock, knock.

                Silence.

LILY   Murray?

MURRAY   Yup .

LILY   You gave me quite a start.

MURRAY   Sorry, Miss. I never thought.

LILY   What are you doing here at this hour, shouldn't you be getting ready for church?

MURRAY   No, Miss. We don't attend.

LILY   *(dry)* Smart.

                ROSE comes bursting in from the shadows behind MURRAY.

ROSE	LILY
We used to go, but Daddy lost belief.	Jesus!

MURRAY   No, I never. You hush, Rose. I've got my own ways. *(beat)* Sorry, Miss. We didn't mean to startle ya.

LILY   It's alright. I just wasn't expecting anyone. The guys in the band clear out pretty quickly after the last set, but sometimes I like to stay and watch the sun come up.

MURRAY	ROSE
I know.	That's the best way to say hello to God, isn't it?

LILY   Yes. Yes, it is. I never thought of it that way.

ROSE   He lives in the lake, doesn't He, Daddy?

MURRAY   So they say.

ROSE	He lives in everything. In every living thing. That's why we don't have to go to church; we can talk to God without a preacher.

ROSE holds out a wildflower.

ROSE	This is for you.

LILY takes the flower.

LILY	Where did you find this?
ROSE	Growing along the road by the lake.
LILY	It's beautiful. Thank you. *(beat)* How did you know I'd be here to give it to?

ROSE blushes and looks to MURRAY.

ROSE	The god in the lake told me to–
MURRAY	*(interrupts)* We were goin' down to the pier to start the boat for the mornin' run up the lake to Brown's when I seen yer husband, Lloyd, sitting down there on his wheelchair.
LILY	Lloyd? *(beat)* Oh, Jesus, he was supposed to wait at home.

She goes to the window and looks down to the pier.

MURRAY	Sure. He's been sittin' down there ever since I brung him up the lake, about nine o'clock last night. I wouldn't worry about him, though; I've been keepin' an eye on him; I even went down a couple times last night and asked him why he didn't just come on inside like everybody else?
	(beat) He's been drinkin' a lot, eh? Cursin' and drinkin' an' playin' along with you on his clarinet; he never missed a song, all night. *(beat)* Crazy, eh?
LILY	Something like that. I'd better scoot.

> *LILY starts to go.*

MURRAY   Oh, I'd leave him out there to sober up; I'd let him cool down a bit if I was you. We'll take him in the boat with us when we go; tell him how great you were last night; how me an' Rose walked ya home alone to The Hiawatha right after the show. *(beat)* I hate people when they're actin' crazy; they scare the bejesus outta' me.

> *Pause.*

ROSE   I'm named after you.

LILY   Is that so?

MURRAY   *(embarrassed)* Well, ya both got the name of flowers.

> *LILY laughs.*

ROSE   An' we were watchin' you through the crack in the door 'cause I wanted to see the lady I'm named after, an' Daddy said we could, but only this once, but he bumped the door an' made a noise, so we hadta open it.

MURRAY   We were not spyin'. You quit lyin', Rose.

ROSE   I'm not lyin'.

MURRAY   Yes, ya are. Now you go on down to the boat an' start bailin'.

ROSE   But, Daddy...

MURRAY   I said, git goin' or I'll send ya home an' never bring ya out for the mornin' run up the lake again.

ROSE   But I never...

MURRAY   Rose, I mean it. God says lyin's a sin, an' you lied. Now get.

ROSE runs out the door. It creaks and slams shut behind her.

Kids, eh?

Pause.

LILY   Thanks.

MURRAY   For what?

LILY   The advice. No sense in upsetting him any further. What's a little white lie?

MURRAY   A little white lie.

They both laugh.

In the distance, LLOYD, down on the pier, starts to play "It's A Sin To Tell A Lie."

LILY laughs and begins to sing along with the clarinet, teasing MURRAY.

After a verse or two, she sprawls out on the floor in front of him like a big cat, laughing at her own joke.

Pause.

I remember you from school up at Watrous, before you went away to be a singer. *(beat)* I remember when ya left here. Boy, did people talk. *(He laughs.)* It's no wonder ya stayed away so long. You couldn'ta come back if ya wanted. At least not until ya got famous enough ta rub it in their noses.

LILY   Rub their noses in it.

MURRAY   Whatever.

Pause.

LILY   I didn't, you know.

MURRAY   What?

LILY   Come back to rub their noses in it.

MURRAY   I know.

LILY   What do you know?

MURRAY   Why you come back.

LILY   You do, do you?

MURRAY   Yeah. I do. *(beat)* Ya come back because ya couldn't stay away.

LILY   I came back because my husband is ill.

MURRAY   An' ya knew that ya could bring him back here an' the lake would help him get better. Little Manitou's a sanctuary; maybe it doesn't look like Eden in the *Bible*, but it's an Eden just the same. Where else could ya see a blade a grass throw a shadow five feet long?

LILY   I know.

MURRAY   I know ya know. That's why ya come back.

LILY   I know.

MURRAY   Told ya, didn't I?

LILY   Yes, you did. I suppose you did, yes.

          She gets up and goes to the window overlooking the lake

LILY   It's so beautiful. The lake. So blue against the brown of the hills. *(beat)* It's funny how smooth they look.

MURRAY   They're not, ya know.

LILY	I know. Lloyd and I took the train out from Chicago. It's a lot slower than coming out by car, but it's easier for him to travel that way now. We used to drive everywhere... St. Louis. New Orleans. New York. Once we even drove all the way to Mexico City, just like a couple of outlaws, then all the way back home to Chicago. But you know what's funny? On all those car trips I never once saw the land as clearly as I saw it from the train. And you know what? It scared me. It scared the living daylights out of me to see how the hills are covered with rose bushes and thistle and little bits of shattered rock, and how everything is dried up, stunted, twisted out of shape because the sky is lying right on top of it.
MURRAY	*(entranced)* I like drivin' over the prairie in a car. It makes ya feel real small, like a mouse runnin' over a turtle's back.

       Pause.

I should be headin' out soon.

LILY	Don't hurry away on my account.
MURRAY	I'm not. It's just... what about...?

       He nods toward ROSE and LLOYD, down at the pier.

LILY	It's alright. Rose is probably teaching him how to skip rocks.

       Pause.

MURRAY	I better go.

       Pause.

I never been anyplace else like you have. Well, nowhere special like Chicago or New York City. But I can tell ya that this place is special, too, an' that's why ya can feel the sky lyin' right on top of ya. But

it's a good lyin' on top of ya, like at night when ya
were a kid an' ya'd scare yerself an' then pray ta
Jesus an' He'd come an' cover ya all over with a
warm blanket of love.

LILY   I see.

MURRAY   I know ya do, Miss.

LILY   Lily.

MURRAY   Alright. Lily. I like that. Lily. *(beat)* Lily. *(beat)*
I never knew anybody famous. *(beat)* But you
don't count, do ya, 'cause I already knew ya before.
Well, sort of. I seen ya around here anyway, when
we were kids. Up at school, or down at the east
beach, or smokin' cigarettes with the older guys
down under the lattice work below here at
Danceland. *(beat)* An' late one night when I was
about twelve, I seen ya lyin' all alone on the pier
an' I thought to myself that all the soundsa the
dancin' an' the music floatin' outta' here in
Danceland was just a dream an' here we were, the
only two souls in the universe an' both of us hearin'
the same things, just like Adam an' Eve.

LILY   Nothing but silence mixing with the music of the
spheres.

                Silence.

MURRAY   Was it hearin' the music that made ya want to be a
dancehall singer, or didja always want ta be one?

LILY   Always.

                She pulls out a pack of smokes.

                Want one?

MURRAY   Oh, no. Thank you, Miss... Lily.

LILY   Oh, come on. You smoke. I've seen you lots of
times. Have a smoke with me, then you can take
Lloyd on up to Brown's with you.

Pause.

MURRAY takes a cigarette.

MURRAY   Thanks.

Pause.

LILY lights their smokes.

Did you really see me lots of times?

LILY   Sure. You're always driving past me in your boat.

MURRAY   I know. I always see you walkin' along the shore.

LILY   Then you should wave, silly.

MURRAY   I wanted to a coupla times, but you always looked like you wanted to be alone, so I never.

LILY   Well, next time wave.

Pause.

MURRAY   Where else didja see me?

LILY   I don't know. Lots of places.

MURRAY   Like where?

LILY   All over. At the train station in Watrous.

MURRAY   Where else?

LILY   What's this?

MURRAY   Just tell me where ya seen me like I told where I seen you.

LILY   Alright. I've seen you driving down the lake in your boat; I've seen you picking up passengers with your car at the train station; and late the other night I saw you out in the middle of the lake, diving naked off your boat and playing like a dolphin in the moonlight.

MURRAY I know. I seen ya watchin' me. I wanted ta swim over to ya an' talk, but I was too embarrassed, so I just stayed in the lake, swimmin' an' playin', until ya left an' went back inta here, in Danceland.

LILY I knew you'd seen me. That's why I stayed so long. *(beat)* You surprise me.

MURRAY Do I?

LILY Oh, yes. Oh, yes, you do.

> *She moves away from him.*
>
> *Pause.*

MURRAY So, we're even, eh?

LILY How so?

MURRAY You were watchin' me just like I watched you that night when I was twelve.

LILY I suppose so. But we're not children anymore, are we?

> *Pause.*

MURRAY Do ya like watchin' people?

LILY Sometimes.

MURRAY Me, too.

> *Pause.*

Didja ever see yerself? Like turn around an' see yerself comin' up behind ya?

LILY I don't think so, no.

MURRAY   I did. Once when I was twenty four. An' it sure did surprise me 'cause mostly I just keep an eye out for what others are doin', eh?

> *LILY laughs. MURRAY catches her gently by the jaw.*

No. Really. Don't laugh.

> *He releases her.*

One night I couldn't sleep, an' then just before dawn I got up an' went for a walk. Just ta see the sun comin' up an' to hear the birds start ta singin'. An' I walked along here by the lake' an' nobody else was around, just like this mornin'. An' I walked an' walked, an' said a little prayer ta the Lord ta thank him for all the beauty an' such around me, an' then I sat down on this big rock beside the lake, just lookin' at the sun comin' up an' at the water movin' by, an' then I just kinda fell asleep but my eyes were open an' I could see everything but I was asleep, sittin' there lookin' out at nature, when all of a sudden this snake slithers outta' the grass right in fronta me. It was just a garter snake, right. That's the only kind we got here, so it never scared me or nothin', it just got my attention real quick. So I looked up, an' there I was, walkin' down the path toward myself. *(beat)* I guess that snake startled me an' my body woke up before my soul could get back into it. An' it's a lucky thing, too, it was a snake I seen, an' not a person, 'cause if a person crosses yer path while yer soul's outta' yer body they can snap the little thread that keeps it connected, an' then yer soul can't find ya, an' it hasta spend all eternity roamin' around, lookin' for ya, so it can get back into ya through yer eyeballs, which is where it come out. *(beat)* So that made me start thinkin' about havin' a soul, an' bein' one a God's children, but still bein' a part of the animal world, too, an' how sometimes things mean things. I mean, they can't happen all by themselves, can they?

LILY	No. They can't.
	Pause.
	How old's your daughter?
MURRAY	Twelve.
LILY	Where's her mother?
MURRAY	I dunno. Up north, prob'ly, I don't know.
LILY	Why didn't she take the child?
MURRAY	She did. Sort of. For a while, anyway. Then she brought it back home an' took back off with some guy from Battleford, who works at The Sask. *(beat)* Crazy, hunh? *(beat)* She was an Indian. *(beat)* So after that, I hadta look after Rose. An' my Mom said she'd help; that yer life is yer life, an' yer child is yer child, an' shouldn't be made ta be brought up in the ways of strangers. *(beat)* That's why we don't go to church anymore. *(beat)* 'Cause of all the gossip goes on. *(beat)* So, I'm not really married anymore. Well, I am, but just sorta.
	He moves to LILY.
	Pause.
	You're the one who's married.
LILY	Sort of.
	Silence.
MURRAY	Look. The sky's turnin' inside out.
LILY	Yes. Dawn.
	MURRAY moves in behind her. They both gaze out the window.
MURRAY	The whole sky looks like it's turned inside out, an' yer lookin' down at islands in the ocean.

LILY   How do you know what the ocean looks like?

MURRAY   I don't. But I can imagine.

LILY   I'll bet you can.

MURRAY   I love imaginin'. It's my favourite thing ta do; besides watchin' people. An' every day, winter an' summer, all year long, year after year, ya can look at the sky an' imagine it's... a very beautiful woman.

                Pause.

                He begins to nibble on her neck and fondle her breasts.

                Pause.

                LILY moves away from him and stubs out her cigarette.

LILY   I've been watching you.

MURRAY   I know. I seen ya doin' it.

LILY   I know. I've seen you see me.

                She moves into his arms and they begin to make love as they dance.

MURRAY   When I see my arms goin' around your shoulder blades I feel like I'm holdin' bird bones. My arms look bigger than they really are, an' my veins stick out all blue an' muscley the way I always think a man's arms should look an' mine never do.

LILY   Sssssssshhhhhh! Don't talk.

                She pushes his shirt up off his chest and nuzzles on his nipples and belly.

MURRAY   Mmmmmmm. So soft. So soft.

*He lifts her face to his, and they exchange long,
deep kisses.*

*He undoes her dressing gown and starts to kiss
her breasts.*

*The door swings open and ROSE comes running
into the dancehall.*

ROSE   Mr. Lloyd says to…

*She stops dead in her tracks, turns and heads back
to the door.*

MURRAY   *(bellows)* Rose! You get back here. You sit.

He points to the ground at his feet.

ROSE heels like an obedient dog.

MURRAY   Now you stay put. What did you see?

ROSE   Nothin'.

MURRAY   Were you spyin'?

ROSE   No.

MURRAY   Don't lie, Rose. Were you spyin'?

LILY   It's alright, Murray. She wasn't spying, were you
Rose?

ROSE   No, Miss.

MURRAY   Are ya sure? Are ya sure ya never seen us neckin'?

ROSE   No.

MURRAY   Good. Or else I'll take ya out an leave ya at the side
a the road fer, fer that that American fella… unh,
unh, Dillinger, yeah, Dillinger, ta git.

ROSE   *(terrified)* Don't, Daddy. Don't.

MURRAY   He's... he's hidin' up at Bienfait. I... I seen him
              myself. A little guy in a hat an' glasses. An
              American fella. An' he comes up here lookin' fer
              little girls who spy, an' he picks them up off the
              side a the road an' takes them away ta feed to his
              dogs.

ROSE   I wasn't spyin'. Honest.

LILY   You're scaring her, Murray, so stop it. It's alright
              honey, your Daddy didn't mean to scare you, did
              you Murray?

MURRAY   No. But if yer lyin', Rose, yer gonna' git such a
              hidin'.

ROSE   You're the liar, Daddy! You're the liar!

MURRAY   Ohhh. I am not. I am not.

                    He starts to move in on ROSE.

LILY   Murray, Dillinger's dead and you know it. Some
              woman saw him coming out of a movie theatre in
              Chicago last month and called the cops. They set
              up an ambush and shot him down.

MURRAY   An' he had his face changed, so how do you know
              it was really him that they shot down?

LILY   Oh, come on...

MURRAY   An' how come the Mounties been around lookin'
              for an American fella they say did the killin' up in
              Bienfait last week? Why'd anybody except Dillinger
              wanna' come all the way up here just ta do a killin'
              when there's plenty ta do right at home in the
              States? No. No, it was him I seen. I know it. He's
              here. He's here hidin' out again, just like he does
              every summer, an' he'll git ya Rose if ya don't
              come over here right now an' take a good lickin'.

                    ROSE shrieks and clings to LILY for safety.

ROSE	Noooooooooooooooooo!
LILY	Don't frighten the child.
MURRAY	Don't tell me how ta raise my daughter.
LILY	I'm not telling you how to…
MURRAY	You don't even have one, so how would you know how to raise it?
LILY	Because I remember what it felt like to be one!
MURRAY	Rose! Git over here right now, I'm gonna' tan yer hide for disobedience!

       ROSE clings harder to LILY.

ROSE	Noooooooooooooooooo!
MURRAY	I said, git over here!

       He grabs ROSE from LILY, and throws the child across the floor.

       LILY and ROSE scream together…

LILY & **ROSE**	Noooooooooooooooooooooooooooooooooooooooo!

       The child hits the floor, and MURRAY pulls his belt out of his belt loops in a single motion.

       LILY lunges at him and grabs his upraised arm.

       MURRAY stops dead. Surprised by her strength.

LILY	I'll tell you something, Murray. Dillinger's not dead. I lied. He did have his face changed. Then he drove twelve hundred miles up here with the FBI on his tail, because he's a friend of mine and he knew I'd help him out. That's his white Chevy convertible that's been parked out behind The Hiawatha Hotel all week. He hides out in my dressing room.

So if you lay so much as one finger on that child, or mention so much as one word about what went on in here this morning, I'm going to whisper in his ear what a dangerous son of a bitch you really are, and he'll hunt you down and put a bullet through your brain just like he did to that poor bastard of a union man up in Bienfait last week.

Silence.

MURRAY   C'mon, Rose. We gotta' go.

He hoists ROSE up off the floor and hurries to the door.

As he gets there, he turns back to LILY.

MURRAY   We'll take yer husband, Lloyd, with us, too. There's no point in his waitin' around all mornin' for an adulteress.

MURRAY and ROSE plunge through the doors and run down to the pier.

Sunlight blasts past them until the double doors slam shut.

LILY is in a state of shock.

LILY   *(quietly)* Jesus Christ!

Fade Out.

— — Scene Three — —

Fade in.

LLOYD's cabin.

Early afternoon. Sunday.

It is extremely hot.

> *LLOYD is alone, sharing a couple of stiff cocktails with himself and working on some new arrangements. He hums a few notes, then tries to write them down. He's not being too successful and is getting frustrated. He snaps his pencil in half and slams back a couple belts of rye.*

LLOYD   Jazz. Christ. What a life.

> *He tosses his sheet music into the air. It falls down around him like snowflakes.*
>
> *He hears footsteps approaching.*

LILY   *(off)* Lloyd?

> *LLOYD wheels away into a dark corner.*
>
> *We hear the persistent drone of flies.*
>
> *LILY enters, carrying a couple of small suitcases.*

LILY   Lloyd?

> *Silence.*
>
> *She puts the suitcases down, then starts to pick up the sheafs of sheet music.*

LLOYD   *(from the shadows)* Looking for something?

LILY   Lloyd!?

LLOYD   Surprise, surprise.

LILY   You're here.

LLOYD   I live in this hovel, you're the one has to stay in a fancy hotel.

LILY   Nice to see you, too. You're in a good mood.

LLOYD   I don't have moods.

LILY	Good. Neither do I. *(beat)* Are these your new arrangements? I told the boys in the band I'd work with them later today.
LLOYD	Oh, you did, did you? And where do I fit into these plans?
LILY	Well... you don't. It's my band.
LLOYD	And they're my arrangements.
LILY	I know, but it's our night off and we've been playing the same tunes for two weeks now, we need some new material. I just thought I'd take them down to Danceland and run through them a couple of times.
LLOYD	Well, think again, Missy. Think again.
LILY	But you wrote them for me.
LLOYD	I wrote them for me. They're my ticket out of here and I'm not giving them to anybody unless I get to see a substantial part of the action. Those clowns in your band can't even read. You think I want people hearing farmers play my arrangements?
LILY	They're not farmers. They're from Saskatoon.
LLOYD	Same difference. They're so white they're almost blue. Who the hell do you think you are, leaving me stranded on a pier...
LILY	I didn't leave you stranded...
LLOYD	...in the middle of hell's half acre all night...
LILY	I didn't even know you were there!
LLOYD	...and then come waltzing in here to steal my arrangements as if nothing happened?
LILY	I wasn't stealing your arrangements; I was just going to borrow them!

LLOYD	Borrow! Is that what you call it? Borrow? Right. And teach them to a bunch of thieving musicians; the next thing I know I'm hearing my tunes on the radio and haven't got a penny to show for it. Six months work spread around as free and easy as a case of crabs.
LILY	Don't be so vulgar.
LLOYD	Oh, I forgot. You regained your virginity when we crossed the border.
LILY	Stop it, Lloyd, I'm sick of it. You throw a jealous conniption fit at least twice a day!
LLOYD	I do not!
LILY	Yes, you do. You haven't let up on me since we got here. Two whole weeks.
LLOYD	And I've got seven more weeks to go; day after day cooped up in this Hades hot cabin listening to the goddamned flies ricochet off the screens while you stay up in town screwing around with the local playboys.
LILY	I am not screwing around with the local...
LLOYD	Murray told me he saw some man hiding in your dressing room this morning.
LILY	That's stupid, Lloyd. How could Murray see somebody who wasn't there?
LLOYD	Maybe he's clairvoyant.
LILY	That's a laugh.
LLOYD	If that sucker had half a brain it'd be lonely, but he doesn't have any reason to lie to me. He came running out of Danceland this morning as if he'd seen the Devil himself. He practically kidnapped me off the pier. I wanted to stay and spend the morning at the hotel with you, but he wouldn't let me. He was

	stuttering away and his daughter was crying; they drove me up the lake like a bat out of hell and dumped me out on the beach. I had to crawl up for help to push this goddamned wheelchair through the sand and I want to know where the hell you've been!
LILY	Packing! Getting ready to move out here with you, alright?!
LLOYD	Murray says Dillinger's here…
LILY	Dillinger!
LLOYD	…and The Mounties are looking for him.
LILY	For the last time, Lloyd, Dillinger's dead!
LLOYD	That's why you stayed up at Danceland all night isn't it? The papers say he had his face changed.
LILY	For God's sake, calm down. You're hysterical.
LLOYD	I AM NOT HYSTERICAL! I took a bullet in the belly from that son of a bitch, and I am not hysterical!
LILY	WE WERE SHOOTING COCAINE, WE WERE NOT SCREWING! It's not my fault you came busting into a private hotel room. He thought you were a cop. Jealousy, Lloyd! One of these days it's going to kill you. *(beat)* I was at the hotel. Packing. Alright? Either accept my word on it or I'll pack your waxy old carcass back onto the train to Chicago.
LLOYD	You wouldn't dare.
LILY	Just watch me. *(beat)* I don't know why I didn't dump you years ago.
LLOYD	Because you needed my talent; you still do!
LILY	I don't believe this.

LLOYD   I made you who you are and now that I'm a cripple, you just shuck me off onto the floor like a used rubber. Hell, the maid'll be around in the morning to pick me up. *(beat)* You sucked my talent like a vampire. Sometimes when we'd make love, your hands felt like claws in my back, and I'd hear your tongue so loud in my ear, sucking and sucking, trying to suck the music right out of my brain, and I'd know you needed me and I'd know you hated me for it.

LILY   You're wrong about when I started to hate you. *(beat)* It didn't start in bed. I might have needed you, and God knows I worshipped your talent, worshipped it to the point where I didn't think I had any myself.

LLOYD   Oh, come on...

LILY   I started to hate you started to hate you the moment you walked into that hotel room in Chicago.

LLOYD   So what was I supposed to do?

LILY   The look on your face...

LLOYD   ...keep on playing blackjack...

LILY   ...you were purple with rage...

LLOYD   ...down in the bar?

LILY   JEALOUSY, LLOYD! JEALOUSY!

LLOYD   YOU WERE MY WIFE!

LILY   You were shouting...

LLOYD   I LOVED YOU!

LILY   You were shouting...

LLOYD   I loved you!

LILY You took away my choice.

LLOYD I loved you.

LILY You destroyed my freedom. *(beat)* You have no idea what you walked in on. The freedom. The possibilities. To be in that room with that man. To be sitting there with John Dillinger, the most dangerous man in the world... I was flying. I was free. Maybe just for a minute. Maybe just for a couple of hours, but Jesus Christ, I could have been free and if a person can't be free in this life, even if it's only for long enough to feel an assassin's bullet in your brain, then it sure as hell isn't worth living. *(beat)* You're not the man I married. You've become unbelievably cruel. I did not suck your talent. You were thirty-four when we met; I was only sixteen, what did I know? I'd run away from home. I'd only been in Chicago for ten days!

LLOYD Exactly my point.

LILY What?!

LLOYD Who ever heard of a singer being from Saskatchewan? Nobody. That's who. Until I picked you up and made you who you are.

LILY I am who I am because of me, not because of you, so don't patronize me, you bastard.

LLOYD *(mimics)* Don't patronize me, you bastard. Just fuck me and make me famous.

LILY *(beat)* You self-pitying parasite. If you'd just stop feeling sorry for yourself you might make something of yourself again. But, oh, no. You'd rather cripple around in your wheelchair, whining and complaining.

LLOYD I DO NOT WHINE!

LILY Yes, you do. YOU WHINE! You do nothing but whine and bitch and feel sorry for yourself. You're an emotional cripple, Lloyd, and I'm not going to take it. You like being sick. You like being a cripple. You like it because it makes you feel as if you have control over me again, just like when we first met.

LLOYD   Control?! Control?! Nobody could control you. You screwed every musician and criminal in the Midwest!

LILY   SO?! *(beat)* You know something, Lloyd? You're right. I have needs. Sexual needs. Remember?

LLOYD   Who cares?

LILY   I care! And so should you!

LLOYD   Alright! So why don't you just diddle me and get it over with; just quit all this yip, yip, yip!

LILY   *(to herself)* Christ.

              Silence.

LLOYD   *(lost)* I don't know what I'd do without you, alright?

              Pause.

LILY   You'd manage.

LLOYD   Probably. But I wouldn't like it.

LILY   Why not? Nobody to boss around?

LLOYD   Naah. Nobody to dance with. *(beat)* You're a swell dancer.

              Pause.

              (subdued) I'm sorry.

LILY   *(beat)* Just be stronger, alright?

LLOYD   Alright. I promise. *(beat)* I treasure you.

LILY   Don't treasure me, Lloyd. Just love me. *(beat)* Just love me the way you used to.

> *Pause.*

LLOYD   I love you, Lily. I really do.

> *Silence.*

C'mon. *(beat)* Dance with me.

LILY   You're kidding.

LLOYD   I never kid about dancing.

> *Pause.*

> *LLOYD, very slowly and with considerable pain, draws himself up onto his feet.*

> *He stands for a moment, unsure if he can support himself.*

> *Then he gains his footing and reaches out to her.*

C'mon. Just once. For old time's sake.

> *She goes to him and takes his hands, supporting his weight.*

(beat) We had some times, hunh?

> *They start to dance; a slow, close waltz.*

> *After awhile, LLOYD begins to sing very softly to her.*

> *LILY joins him. Their voices blend in perfect harmony.*

> *By the time they finish the tune, they are laughing and kissing.*

> *The laughter subsides.*

Silence.

Oh, baby, I've gotta' siddown.

> *LILY slowly lowers him back down into his wheelchair.*

LILY   You're getting better, Lloyd. Come on, let's spend some time in the lake, take a mudbath down on the shore.

LLOYD   Don't be ridiculous. No goddamned magic mud is going to get me another band like The Dawn Patrol Boys.

LILY   *(beat)* The mud isn't magic. It's got minerals in it.

LLOYD   Who cares, it's still mud.

LILY   I know, but it's special mud. Like at Karlsbad, in Germany.

LLOYD   Maybe the idea of a mudbath sounds better in Kraut.

LILY   Maybe it does. *(beat)* Look. It's simple. You cover yourself in mud and then let the sun bake it onto your skin; it pulls all the poisons out of you. Then you go for a long, salty swim in the lake and wash it off, and then you do it again and again, all day long, all summer long.

LLOYD   I know. I just feel really stupid sitting around all covered with mud in a wheelchair at the beach.

LILY   Well, don't take the wheelchair, silly. Use your crutches. *(beat)* C'mon, let's go. I'll limp, so that when we get there you can say the crutches are mine.

> *She goes to get some towels and their swimwear.*

When I was walking out here I found some long salt crystals down on the beach. They must have

been six or seven inches long. I was going to bring
them to you, but I was afraid they'd turn to dust in
my pocket.

*She hands him his trunks and a towel, then starts
to undress him.*

Little Manitou's a sanctuary; an Eden. It's where
I grew up; where I'm from. *(beat)* When we were
kids we'd come out here on winter evenings and
toboggan down the ravine over by Winnipeg Street,
or go skating out on the lake. And afterwards, all
the families would gather at the hotel. Not The
Hiawatha. The other one. The old one. I forget what
it was called. It burnt down. *(beat)* The hotels at the
lake are always burning down.

LLOYD is naked now.

LLOYD   God, you're something.

Pause.

He crawls into his trunks.

LILY   It's even more beautiful here in the winter than in
the summer. Everything takes on the colour of the
sky and the sun; everything turns mauve and pink
and blue, every shade of blue; except the hills. The
wind blows all the snow down into drifts on the
lake and the hills stay as bare and brown in the
winter as they do in the summer. It sweeps the
snow back off their brows like my mother used to
sweep the hair back off my forehead. *(pause)*
I remember winter nights when the boys would
come down from Watrous to play hockey. We'd all
tell our moms we were coming down to practice
figure skating, but we weren't. We were coming
down to watch the boys get rough with each other.
And sometimes, after they'd played for awhile,
we'd snuggle down with them in the snowdrifts
under the lattice work at Danceland and smoke
cigarettes; and maybe one of the older boys, one
of the tough ones, would neck with you.

She hands LLOYD his crutches.

He takes them from her, then lowers them down onto the floor.

He reaches out and gently caresses her as she talks.

It's funny, you know. I remember one night; after chores; after supper, in the dark; after the boys had come down and shovelled the snow off the ice, they brought down this can of gasoline and poured it out, all over their hockey rink. Then they had everybody stand back and one of them, one of the older guys, I forget his name, he was a great kisser, he's a farmer now, lit a match and tossed it out onto the ice. The whole lake seemed to explode. The flames must have been ten feet high, and they burned like hell for about a minute and a half; they actually set the ice on fire and scorched the snow-drifts at the side of the rink. I'll never forget it. They actually burned the snow. And we all just stood and watched, horrified, but fascinated, because we knew the fire couldn't go anywhere; it was so hot and contained that it had to burn itself out. And when it was over, except for a few patches of flame, lingering in the corners, the lake ice was covered with a thin film of water. And we watched as it froze; it only took about another minute; it's so cold here in the winter. And then, when it was frozen, mirror perfect, you could see the stars reflected in it, the boys rushed out onto the ice and started gouging and chipping away at it with the heels of their skateblades. And I jumped out, too. Not to wreck it, but to protect it; to keep it perfect; just one tiny corner of the ice rink. And when the boys would swoop past me on their skates, I'd slam my elbow into their ribs; I learned that from watching them play hockey; and they'd fall down and then get up and glide to their buddies; and it happened again and again, a half dozen times, until they formed a gang and came sweeping down the ice toward me, and I started jumping up and down, doing it myself, gouging and chipping away with the heel of my skateblade, better than any one of them could have done. *(beat)* I never understood why I did that, I guess I just felt that if something perfect was going to be destroyed, I'd rather do it myself. *(beat)* There's a power here; in this valley. Where else could you see a blade of grass throw a shadow five feet long?

LLOYD   I don't know.

LILY   Neither do I.

LLOYD   *(beat)* C'mon. I'm just about ready for that mudbath.

LILY   Good. Let's go, then.

She reaches up and gently caresses his face.

LILY   When it gets dark, I'll show you how the sky turns inside out.

She puts her arms around him and they head for the door.

Fade out.

— — *Scene Four* — —

Danceland.

Dusk. Sunday.

Deep mauve light spills in through the curtains. Gold light flows in under the doors.

ROSE is wearing LILY's dressing gown.

She is entertaining MURRAY. The two of them are convulsed with laughter.

As their laughter subsides, MURRAY speaks.

MURRAY   Do it again, Rose.

ROSE   Nooooo, Daddy.

MURRAY   Rose…. C'mon, be Lily again.

ROSE   No, Daddy.

MURRAY   C'mon, Rose, you do her so good. *(beat)* Rose. *(beat)* Be Lily again.

ROSE   Don't be monkeynuts, Daddy. It's gettin' dark out an' people'll be comin'.

MURRAY   Please. I'll watch the door, Rose. Please.

ROSE   I am too named after her.

MURRAY   I know that. Jeez. *(He sings softly…)* Weatherman, Weatherman…

ROSE   *(beat)* Alright. But just one more time.

MURRAY   Okay. Then we'll put her nightie thing back in her dressing room.

ROSE   *(reluctant)* Alright.

MURRAY   Good girl.

> *He gives her a kiss. Then she starts to sing*

ROSE   Weatherman… Weatherman… Weatherman…

> *MURRAY sings along, lost in his own fantasy world.*

**ROSE &
MURRAY**   Weatherman…

> *MURRAY stops singing. ROSE continues.*
>
> *MURRAY looses a hideous growl and chases ROSE, both of them screaming with laughter, through the deserted dancehall.*

He catches her from behind, hoists her up into the air above him, laughing and growling. He strips the dressing gown off her and then pretends to eat her alive.

They collapse into a jumble of arms, legs, laughter and tears Eventually they both calm down a bit.

ROSE   I love you, Daddy.

MURRAY   I love you, too, Rose.

Pause.

Then ROSE tries to pull the dressing gown away from him. MURRAY grabs at it. It rips.

Silence.

MURRAY   Oh, no. No. You ripped it. You ripped her nightie thing.

Pause.

Oh, she's gonna' know. She's gonna' think I ripped it. You see what you did?

ROSE   We could take it away with us and then she'll think somebody stole it.

MURRAY   Oh, that's bad. That's bad. That's stealin'. Really. Don't you ever steal. No. I'm gonna' hafta say I ripped it. I'm gonna' hafta lie for ya, and there's a worse punishment for lyin' than there is for stealin'. YOU SEE WHAT YOU DID?!

MURRAY growls and lunges at ROSE. She curls up in a little ball.

ROSE   Mmmmooooommmmmmeeeeeee!

MURRAY steps dead in his tracks. He picks up the dressing gown and disappears into LILY's dressing room.

Silence.

ROSE   *(whimpers)* Mommy? Mommy?

Silence.

ROSE looks up. She is alone.

Daddy? *(beat)* Daddy? *(beat)* Daddy, where are you?

Silence.

Daddy, where are you?

Pause.

C'mon, Daddy I know you're there.

Silence.

I didn't mean to do it, so come on out, Daddy. *(beat)* I'm goin' home, Daddy. *(beat)* Daddy, I'm goin' home now.

Silence.

Daddy?

Silence.

(shrieks) Daaaaaaaaaaaaaaaaaadddddeeeeeeeeeeeeeeeee!

She runs out of the dancehall. The doors slam shut behind her.

Silence.

MURRAY enters from the gloom of the dressing room, still holding LILY's silk dressing gown. He calls after ROSE...

MURRAY   Scaredycat!

Silence.

Murray is lost in thought.

He runs his hand over the dressing gown, enjoying the smooth feel of the silk. Then he lifts it to his face and inhales deeply.

MURRAY Mmmmmm. So good. Perfume and talcum powder and flower petals.

He inhales its fragrance again.

So pretty. Aren't you the pretty one? Prettier even than when I used to watch you up at school in Watrous.

He goes to the window and peers out. Nobody's there. Then he crosses to the door and quickly peeks out through the keyhole. Again, nobody's there.

MURRAY undoes the buttons on his shirt and gently rubs the silk across his chest. Eventually, he takes his shirt right off and stops to inhale LILY's scent.

Mmmmm. I can smell ya. Yes, I can. I can smell ya. *(beat)* Can you smell me? Can ya smell my sweat? Can ya? I can smell yours. You're not so clean. Not so pretty that you don't sweat, too. Ya sweat just like me, don'tcha? *(pause)* Does yer husband like the smell of yer sweat? I bet he doesn't. I bet he hasn't smelled ya fer a long time. A long, long time. An' I bet ya miss it. Miss bein' sniffed an' licked the way I could sniff an' lick ya. Oh, yes. Oh, yes, you do. *(beat)* I'm gonna' get ya from him. Yes, I am. I'm gonna' get you for my own. Even if I hafta lie for ya; oh, yeah, I'd lie for ya. Yes, I would. I'd lie ta make you my own.

He kicks off his shoes, then undoes the buttons on his pants and pushes them down around his ankles, all the time rubbing the silk dressing gown on his chest, his stomach, his thighs.

*He straddles the dressing gown and then lies
down on top of it, slowly making love to an
imaginary LILY.*

I love ya, Lily. Yes, I do. I love ya. An' ya want me.
Yeah. Ya do. I know it. Oh, yeah, ya needed me so
bad this mornin'. I could feel ya pressed up against
me, throbbin' an' achin' just like me. An' I needed
ta fill ya up, fill ya up all creamy, an' then feel
myself runnin' sticky back down outta' ya, on your
thighs an' on mine, an' know that when we finished
we'd got each other's shape stored up in our bodies
an' souls, an' we'd always become each other's
shape, whenever we made love, even to other people, 'cause our love would hold, as pure an' strong
as steel. It was. It was when I was smellin' your
hair, an' feelin' your skin an' hearin' your breathin'
so close to the surface that I could tell what you
were thinkin'. Oh, yeah, I could hear your thinkin'
through your breathin'. Yes, I could. I could hear
your thinkin' just as loud as my own.

*A shadow passes over the window, startling
MURRAY.*

Shit. Oh, shit. Shit.

*He frantically attempts to simultaneously disen-
tangle himself from the dressing gown and pull
his pants and shirt back on.*

*Having accomplished most of this, he now doesn't
know what to do with the dressing gown, so he
just chucks it on the floor.*

*He thinks better of this, runs to it, picks it up and
tosses it off into LILY's dressing room.*

Silence.

Somebody rattles the door from the outside.

Who's there? Is that you, honey? Is that you?

He goes to the door and opens it.

Rose? Rose? Hon?

Silence.

MURRAY panics.

He slams the door and bolts it.

Silence.

Dillinger. Shit. He's lookin' for a place ta hide.

The door rattles again.

Murray hunches down onto the floor and begins to crawl toward Lily's dressing room.

He stops dead.

Shit.

He inches back to his shoes, gathers them up and resumes his journey across the floor.

He's comin' in... he's comin' in... he's comin' in....
Oooooh, shit, he's comin' in here... he's comin'...
he's comin'... he's comin'...

A door opens and bangs shut at the back of the dancehall.

MURRAY crouches into a tight little ball. His whimpering punctuates the silence.

A light goes on in LILY's dressing room.

Silence.

MURRAY cowers on the floor.

The light goes out.

The door at the back opens and bangs shut.

Silence.

In the distance, a couple of large dogs bark.

Jesus mercy, Jesus mercy, Jesus mercy

Pause.

He gets up and looks out the window.

Nobody there.

He cautiously exits into LILY's dressing room.

Silence.

Moonlight streams in through the window. The curtains billow gently on the breeze.

(off) It's gone. He took it.

Silence.

MURRAY re-enters.

Why'd Dillinger wanna take her nightie thing? *(beat)* Shit. I bet he's gonna' kill her for screwin' around with another guy; that's what I'd do. I'll bet he's gonna' kill her for screwin' around with... me.

He gathers his courage and moves to the door. Assured that nobody is there, he takes a large breath and then in one movement, unlocks the door and dives headlong into the moonlight.

Lllliiiiiiiiiiiiiiiiillllllllllllleeeeeeeeeeeeeeeee!

His voice echoes across the valley.

The door at the back creaks open and then bangs shut.

> *ROSE enters from the shadows, carrying LILY's dressing gown.*

ROSE   Scaredycat.

> *Fade out.*

ACT TWO

— — *Scene One* — —

> *The cabin.*
>
> *Late evening. Sunday.*
>
> *There's a near empty bottle of whisky sitting on the kitchen table.*
>
> *LLOYD is in his wheelchair, his book of poetry on his lap.*

LLOYD   *(muttering)* Sandburg, Sandburg, Sandburg. Where the hell is Sandburg?

> *He leafs through the book until he finds Sandburg.*

Here it is, here it is. "Limited."

> *He lifts the bottle off the table and takes a long pull off it.*

(pleased as hell) Poetry. Jesus. Nothin' like a bit of poetry for a lonely old bastard who's had too much to drink.

> *He takes another pull off the bottle and reads silently to himself. He is having a wonderful, maudlin time.*
>
> *Pause.*
>
> *LLOYD wipes a tear or two from his cheek, closes the book and takes another pull off the bottle. Then he slams it down onto the table.*
>
> *He wheels over to the window and looks out into the night.*
>
> *After a moment, he lifts his face up to the moon and begins to howl like a lonely wolf, over and over until he starts to laugh.*

*His laughter fills the cabin before it begins to
falter and LLOYD starts to sob.*

*After awhile, his sobbing subsides and he becomes
very still. The moonlight flows in through the
window.*

Pause.

MURRAY comes bursting into the cabin.

MURRAY   Lily! Lily! Lloyd?! Hide! Hide! He's comin'! He's
comin'!

LLOYD   Who's coming?

MURRAY   Dillinger!

LLOYD   *(angry)* Says who?!

MURRAY   Me! Me. I seen him. I seen him myself.

LLOYD   That's what you told me this morning; don't lie to
me. I hate liars!

MURRAY   Lloyd! Lloyd, ya gotta' believe me; I got no reason
to lie to you; I don't lie! I seen him. Seen him
myself; just now; down at Danceland... I... I... I
was down there playin' with Rose... my daughter
Rose... an' we were playin' hide an' seek an' games
an' stuff an' then she got scared one time when I
hid too long an' run home ta my Mom; an' that's
when I seen him. *(beat)* Ohohohoh, I seen his
shadow on the window, then I heard him rattlin'
on the door.

LLOYD   Alright, Murray, just calm down. Just calm down,
now.

Pause.

*MURRAY takes a couple of deep breaths; then he
swallows hard as he remembers why he came.*

MURRAY	Where's Lily?
LLOYD	She's up in town. She said she had a band practice; and she forgot her makeup or some damn thing in her old room at The Hiawatha.
MURRAY	But I checked The Hiawatha, she's not in her room.
LLOYD	*(beat)* I could use another drink.
MURRAY	Me, too, Lloyd. Me, too.
LLOYD	There's a fresh bottle of whisky and a couple of shot glasses in my boot; in the kitchen.

> *MURRAY goes out to pick up the shotglasses and the bottle.*

(mutters) Dillinger. In a pig's eye.

> *MURRAY hightails it back out of the shadows, bottle and shotglasses in hand.*

You did right to come, Murray. So you just sit yourself down here. We're going to drink some whiskey and you're going to tell me exactly what you saw.

> *MURRAY sits.*

> *LLOYD pours him a shot of whiskey and watches while he knocks it back. Then LLOYD pours him another. MURRAY knocks that one back, too.*

> *LLOYD pours himself a shot, downs it, then pours out two more.*

You're alright now. You did right to come. *(beat)* So tell me what you saw.

MURRAY	I was down in Danceland an' it was gettin' dark. An' I seen him pass by the window. That American fella. The one The Mounties been lookin' for, did the killin' up in Bienfait last week. The same one I seen this mornin', sneerin' at me from the shadows

in… in yer wife, Lily's, dressin' room. I seen him
around here a coupla times before, too.

LLOYD   Dillinger?

MURRAY Dillinger.

LLOYD   *(beat)* John Dillinger.

> *Pause.*

> *LLOYD is undergoing a strange transition. His
> voice is filled with a cold, steely anger. He is calm
> and focussed; he suddenly seems dead sober.*

(cold) So you saw him through the window.

MURRAY Then he tried ta get in through the door, only it was
locked 'cause I got scared myself after my little girl
run away.

LLOYD   Is your little girl alright? Is she safe?

MURRAY Jesus. I don't know. I sure hope so. Jesus. Jesus,
I hope so.

LLOYD   Alright, alright. It's alright, Murray. She's probably
safe at home.

MURRAY She must be. Yeah. She must be, 'cause she was
gone about ten minutes before I seen him lookin' in
at me through the window. *(beat)* Oh, God, I hope
so.

LLOYD   So, then what happened? How do you know for
sure it was Dillinger?

MURRAY 'Cause then he come in through the back door, an'
went inta her yer wife, Lily's dressin' room, an'
turned on the light.

LLOYD   Did you see him then? Did you get a look at his
face?

MURRAY	Yeah. Yeah. He was wearin' a hat.
LLOYD	Was he tall or short?
MURRAY	Unh… unh…. Tall!
LLOYD	Liar!

> *MURRAY reaches over and grabs LLOYD by the knee.*

MURRAY	No! No! Short!

> *LLOYD recoils from MURRAY's grasp.*

LLOYD	Don't! Don't touch my legs!
MURRAY	Sorry! Sorry!
LLOYD	Nobody touches my legs!
MURRAY	Sorry!
LLOYD	Just be careful, alright?!
MURRAY	Alright.
LLOYD	Alright.
MURRAY	Sorry.
LLOYD	Stop apologizing!
MURRAY	I said I was sorry!
LLOYD	And I said, shut up!
MURRAY	I am shut up! Jeez, you're not my mom, you know!

> *LLOYD cracks him across the skull.*
>
> *Pause.*

I'm real sorry, Lloyd. I won't touch you no more, okay?

LLOYD Never mind. *(beat)* So then what did he do?

MURRAY He…. He…. He picked up her nightie thing and, oh, God, Lloyd, he was so ugly. His face is all scars where they stitched it back on, and he… he… he was rubbin' her nightie thing on himself. To get the smell. Like a… like a… like an animal. Sniffin' it an' then rubbin' it on himself.

LLOYD *(quiet)* I'm going to kill the bastard.

Pause.

MURRAY I hope ya do kill him, Lloyd. I hope an' pray ya do kill him. He's an animal. Just like an animal. Killin' people an' stealin' their money. An' what he done ta yer wife… ta her… her nightie thing. He's… he's just like an animal.

LLOYD *(very cold)* Shut up and drink your whiskey, Murray.

MURRAY does.

Pause.

Then what did he do?

MURRAY He…. He…. He turned out the light an' he… an' he… he left! *(beat)* I seen it all; I seen his gun. I thought fer sure he was comin' out here in his car, that white Chevy they say he drives; the one's been parked out back of The Hiawatha Hotel all week; comin' out here ta kill her for lockin' him outta' his hidin' place. *(beat)* Oh, God, Lloyd, I hope I'm wrong.

LLOYD Did you see his car when you came in? The Chevy? Did you?

MURRAY No, Lloyd, I never. An' I sure was lookin'.

LLOYD	You came out by boat, didn't you?
MURRAY	Yeah, I…
LLOYD	If he was coming out by car he'd have got here before you, wouldn't he?
MURRAY	Unless he's hidin' in the bushes.
LLOYD	No. He's not hiding in the bushes' Murray. I know Dillinger.
MURRAY	Ya do?
LLOYD	I do. *(beat)* Hotel rooms, Murray. He hides in hotel rooms.
MURRAY	He does?
LLOYD	He does. Which room did you check?
MURRAY	Unh… top floor?
LLOYD	Did you knock?
MURRAY	Nope. I peeked in through the keyhole.
LLOYD	Good move. Never knock on Dillinger's door, the bastard's fast as a rattlesnake.
MURRAY	He is?
LLOYD	He is.
MURRAY	So, where is he?
LLOYD	He's at The Hiawatha Hotel, Murray.
MURRAY	But I checked The Hiawatha…
LLOYD	You didn't check hard enough! *(beat)* Nope. He's at The Hiawatha Hotel in the view room on the top floor at the front with my goddamned whore of a wife. *(beat)* She's gonna' die, too.

MURRAY   Oh, no, Lloyd. Don't kill yer wife. Don't. Just don't, eh?

LLOYD   I'm not gonna', Murray. *(beat)* You are.

                    He wheels away from MURRAY.

MURRAY   Oh, no. No, no. No, no, no, no, no...

                    Pause.

                    LLOYD motions for MURRAY to come to him. MURRAY does.

                    LLOYD pours a couple big slugs of the whisky into their glasses, then tucks the bottle into the side pocket on his wheelchair.

LLOYD   Now you listen, and you listen good. I'm only going to tell you this once. You get it wrong, you're a dead man. You understand?

MURRAY   *(nods)* Sure, Lloyd. Sure. Whatever you want.

LLOYD   Good. This is what we're gonna' do. We're gonna' take this bottle and get back in your boat. We're gonna' fill it with gasoline and stuff a rag in the top. Then we're gonna' get off your boat at the pier below Danceland, just like it's a regular night. Then I'm gonna' hide out inside and you're gonna' go over to The Hiawatha, light the rag on fire and toss it through the window on the top floor at the front where the sinners are sleeping. *(beat)* Hellfire, Murray. You're gonna' flush 'em out with Hellfire. And then you're gonna' come back over to Danceland to help me. You're gonna' help sad old Job turn his pain to joy. We're gonna' wait in the shadows and ambush John Dillinger and his scarlet whore of Babylon.

                    Pause.

MURRAY   Do ya think they'll come?

LLOYD   Where else are they gonna' go?

MURRAY   *(beat)* Okay. Okay, Lloyd. I'll do it.

LLOYD   You're a good man, Murray.

> *LLOYD reaches down and gives MURRAY's shoulder a squeeze.*

Prodigals always come home. *(beat)* Cheers.

MURRAY   Cheers.

> *They clink glasses and shoot back their drinks.*
>
> *LLOYD hands MURRAY the other, empty bottle of whisky.*
>
> *MURRAY gets to his feet. He's nervous, but willing.*

(beat) What if yer wrong, and he's hidin' on the boat?

LLOYD   Then we'll know where he is, won't we? Here. Wait a minute I'll need you to wheel me up from the pier once we get there.

> *LLOYD wheels over to his crutches, hoists himself up onto them and rolls the wheelchair across the floor. The empty wheelchair stops in front of MURRAY: he just stares at it.*
>
> *Pause.*

LLOYD   Just push it for Christ's sake.

MURRAY   I know. I know. Jeez.

> *MURRAY sticks his hand in his pocket and makes a mock gun, which he points at LLOYD.*

Bang, bang, yer dead.

LLOYD   For Christ's sake, Murray, just start the boat, I've
              got you covered.

MURRAY   Sure, Lloyd. Sure. I was just scared, that's all.

              *MURRAY pushes the wheelchair out through the
              door and watches its slow progress through the
              darkness. Then he bolts out after it.*

              *LLOYD watches MURRAY go. Then he looks
              around the room. He hobbles over to the darkened
              kitchen, opens a drawer and pulls a pistol out. He
              tucks it into his belt and heads for the door. On
              his way out, he passes his clarinet. Stops. Picks it
              up.*

LLOYD   Better not forget you. Who knows, I might even
              want to play a little serenade.

              He hobbles out the door, clarinet in hand.

              Fade out.

— — *Scene Two* — —

              Danceland.

              Midnight. Sunday.

              In black...

              *A lonesome, bluesy clarinet wails. A perfect riff.
              Smokey jazz. The sound is coming across the
              water, from LLOYD, who is approaching in
              MURRAY's boat.*

              *Fade in. ROSE, alone in the dancehall. She is
              applying liberal amounts of LILY's white makeup
              to her face.*

              She stops, and starts to pray.

ROSE   The Lord is my shepherd, I shall not want.
He leadeth me beside the still waters
He maketh me to lie down in green pastures.

> *She slowly lies down. Then sits back up again.*

> *She puts on some eyeshadow – her face is begin-*
> *ning to look like a Kabuki mask.*

He maketh me to lie down in green pastures.

> *She slowly lowers herself to the ground again,*
> *then continues the prayer.*

And Yea, though I walk through the valley of the
shadow of death, I shall fear no evil, for The Lord is
my shepherd I shall not want. No!

> *She sits back up again, frustrated because she*
> *can't remember the right words.*

> *She adds a pair of huge red lips to her face mask.*

Thy rod and thy staff, they comfort me? Yes.
Thy rod and thy staff, they comfort me.

> *She stands up and begins to sing "Jesus Loves*
> *Me" in a lewd, bluesy style... emulating LILY's*
> *most provocative stage moves.*

> *ROSE finishes the song, then resumes her*
> *prayers.*

God bless me. God love me. Bless the lake and the
flowers and all the little animals, too. And God?
Bless all the little starving babies. And, God. And,
please, God? If I be good as an angel, let my Mom
come home from livin' in your bosom for ever and
ever Amen.

> *Her mouth drops open just as LLOYD, off in the*
> *approaching boat, lets loose another long, mourn-*
> *ful clarinet wail.*

> ROSE *is surprised, delighted. As if the sound had come from her*

(*awestruck*) Gawd.

> *She lifts her face to the sky and opens her mouth wide.*

> *The clarinet wails again, high and loud.*

(*starting to spin*) I'm an angel. An animal angel. I'm an angel, I'm an angel, I'm an angel.

> *The door at the back of the dancehall creaks open and then bangs shut.*

> ROSE *stops dead. Then she scoops up the makeup and disappears into the shadows.*

> LILY *enters from the dressing room.*

LILY   (*mutters*) Makeup… makeup… where the hell did I leave my makeup?

> *She stops and takes a long, deep breath.*

> *Silence.*

(*low*) Christ it's lonely here. (*beat*) Where's old long dong Dillinger when you really need him?

ROSE   (*from the shadows*) He's dead, Miss. Just like…

LILY   Jesus! What are you doing here?

ROSE   Nothin'.

LILY   (*sees* ROSE's *face*) You little thief. You're the one who took my makeup.

ROSE   No.

LILY   Don't lie to me.

ROSE	I'm not. *(beat)* I'm bein' a lost Assiniboine Princess, crawlin' toward the lake through the fevery night.

> *ROSE gets down on the floor to demonstrate what that might look like. She crawls to LILY and then stops at her feet.*

	Except for me, there's just white people livin' here now. Presbyterians.
LILY	Oh. Them.
ROSE	*(beat)* I want to be like you.
LILY	Oh. *(beat)* No. No, you don't.
ROSE	Yes, I do.
LILY	Whatever for?
ROSE	Because you're like an angel.

> *LILY gently lifts ROSE up off the floor.*

LILY	So are you, sweetheart. So are you.
ROSE	I know. That's why I like you. We're both angels. Animal angels, cryin' for the stars at night.
LILY	Animal angels. Right. Voodoo vixens is more like it. Now let's get you cleaned up and send you home before your Daddy…
ROSE	NO!

> *She jumps back from LILY.*

LILY	Rose? What's the matter?
ROSE	I'm not goin'. I'm stayin' here with you.
LILY	But, honey, it's late…
ROSE	I'm an angel; we're both angels, an' I'm stayin'.

LILY	But people will be worried about you.
ROSE	People should be worried about you.
LILY	What are you talking about?
ROSE	You're all alone an' you shouldn't be. *(beat)* People are comin', I can hear 'em.
LILY	Who?
ROSE	You know. From the lake. I can hear 'em howling like a pack of coyotes pullin' down a deer in a snowdrift.
LILY	Now you're being silly; you're frightening me.
ROSE	But you're an angel, too. Can't you hear 'em?
LILY	No, Rose, I can't. There's nothing to hear; now let's wipe off that makeup and get you home before your Daddy–
ROSE	NO!

>ROSE *crouches low and her mouth drops open.*
>*She is having a seizure.*
>
>LILY *watches as* ROSE *struggles to let her pain*
>*out.*
>
>*Then, from the depths of* ROSE's *belly comes a*
>*cry, low, smokey, bluesy, almost like a clarinet*
>*wail.*
>
>ROSE *subsides onto the floor.*
>
>LILY *goes to* ROSE *and takes her in her arms.*
>ROSE *is sobbing.*
>
>*Eventually* ROSE *becomes very quiet and very*
>*still, slumped in* LILY's *arms.*
>
>*Pause.*

(quiet) Little Manitou was made from angel tears. That's why the lake's so salty; it's made from angel tears just like mine. It's a magic place, and nobody ever drowned here except for one beautiful Assiniboine Princess who could hear the animal angel cry inside her so loud she had to let it out. And her husband heard it and was so scared he beat her up to make it stop. And it did. But then the Princess was so lonely that she wanted to die. Then one night she heard her animal angel again, far away in the distance, just like a lonely coyote crying for the stars at night. But the angel was afraid to come close on account of it didn't want the Princess to get beat up again. So the Princess decided to run away to be with the angel again. And my Daddy said the God in the lake heard her footsteps running across the lake ice, and he couldn't stand for her to leave the valley and him be left livin' all alone, so he reached up through the ice and pulled her down to live in his bosom forever and ever at the bottom of the lake. *(beat)* Don't leave me. Mama, don't leave me. Mama, mama, mama, mama, mama, don't leave me.

> *LILY pulls ROSE close in to her bosom. ROSE begins to calm down.*

LILY   It's alright. I won't leave you. I'll protect you. I won't ever leave you.

ROSE   *(hard)* Yes, you will. And I'll find you in the springtime, just like my Mommy. Starin' up at me through the lake ice, with your hands all tangled up in fishing line.

> *Silence.*

> *The doors to Danceland explode open and LLOYD, in his wheelchair, comes careening into the space.*

> *ROSE bolts through the shadows, out the back door of the dancehall. The front and back doors squeak and bang shut simultaneously.*

LILY	Lloyd?!
	LLOYD wheels around, startled. He pulls the gun on her.
LLOYD	Where the hell is he?
LILY	Who, Lloyd? Who?
LLOYD	Dillinger. That's who.
LILY	Lloyd, put the gun down before you hurt yourself. Nobody's here.
LLOYD	Then who the hell just went scuttling out the back like a shithouse rat?
LILY	Nobody. Rose. *(beat)* Dillinger's dead, Lloyd. I told you. Some woman saw him coming out of a movie theatre...
LLOYD	...don't lie to me...
LILY	...in Chicago last month...
LLOYD	...don't you lie to me...
LILY	...they set up an ambush and shot him down.
LLOYD	...don't you ever lie to me!
LILY	I'm not lying. Why would I lie? *(beat)* Dillinger's dead. Gone. Buried. Kaput. Don't you even read the papers?!
	Silence.
LLOYD	*(low, brutal)* Dance with me.
LILY	You're drunk, Lloyd; imagining things; hallucinating.
LLOYD	SHUT UP! Shut up, shut up, shut up, shut up, shut up!

> *LLOYD draws himself up onto his feet, all the time brandishing the gun in her direction.*
>
> *He stands for a moment, unsure if he can support himself. Then he finds his balance and slowly, with great assurance, points the gun at LILY's head.*

LLOYD *(cold)* I said, dance with me.

> *LILY goes to him He takes her in his arms, the pistol pointed to the back of her neck.*
>
> *They dance in silence.*

What happened to us, Lily?

LILY I feel old when I sleep with you.

> *LLOYD crumples to the floor.*
>
> *Silence.*
>
> *ROSE appears in the doorway of LILY's dressing room.*

There's your John Dillinger, Lloyd. Are you satisfied, now?

LLOYD Oh, Christ.

> *Silence.*

LILY C'mon, Rose. We'd better go.

> *LILY takes ROSE by the hand and they head out.*
>
> *Silence.*

LLOYD Oh, Christ, Lily, come back. Come back, hey? Come back, Lily, I love you. Come back, hey? I love you. I love you, Lily. Come back, hey? *(beat)* You're the cripple. You're the emotional cripple, Lily.

*He sees the bottle of whisky sticking out of the
side pocket of his wheelchair. He crawls over to it
and takes a couple of big slugs.*

I taught you how to backphrase! I taught you how
to sell a tune! *(beat)* Bitch. You weren't so innocent
when we first met.

He takes a couple more pulls off the bottle.

You're the cripple, Lily. You're the emotional cripple. *(beat)* Come back, hey? Come back and let's
make love. *(beat)* Can't love your man anymore.
Can't love the man who loves you because he can't
love you because he's afraid his bones might break.
(beat) But I could kiss you. I could kiss you, and
hold you, and stroke your hair. And if you were
real gentle we could make love, and in our heads it
would be just the same as it was before. Just like
before, when you loved me.

Silence.

The door at the back creaks open.

MURRAY sidles in through the shadows.

MURRAY   Lloyd?

Silence.

I done it, Lloyd. I torched the...

LLOYD   Go to hell.

MURRAY   But, Lloyd, I just torched the...

LLOYD   Get out of here!

MURRAY   What's wrong, Lloyd, should we talk about it?

LLOYD   I said, get out of here!

MURRAY   Okay. Alright. Jeez, whatever ya say, Lloyd.

Pause.

Aren't ya happy now, Lloyd? I thought torchin' The
Hiawatha would make old Job happy.

Pause.

Lloyd?

LLOYD   *(snarls)* What?

MURRAY   Lloyd, I think ya should know…

LLOYD   What?

MURRAY   Fer yer own good…

LLOYD   WHAT?!

MURRAY   Well… well, people are talkin', Lloyd. People are
talkin'.

LLOYD   About what?

MURRAY   About you, Lloyd. About you.

LLOYD   Why would people be talkin' about me, Murray?

MURRAY   I dunno, Lloyd, but I heard 'em. Heard 'em myself.

LLOYD   That's bullshit, Murray, and you know it.

MURRAY   No. No, Lloyd. It's not bull. I'm not lyin'. I was
standin' there watchin' the flames lickin' up the
inside a the curtains on the top floor at the front,
where I tossed the gasoline, when this woman come
up, said she heard glass breakin', an' I said, yeah,
there's a fire goin' on. An' she says, did anybody
tell the people in The Hiawatha or call the fire
brigade, an' I says no, so she run off ta do it herself.
She run off, an' I just stood there starin' at the
flames. I couldn't look away. The Flames A Hell, ya
said; that's where sins get purged. An' I just kept
starin' at 'em thinkin', The Flames A Hell, that's

what they must look like when they're lickin' up ta roast ya. Then the woman comes back an' says, "what're you starin' at?", an' I just said, The Flames A Hell. An' she says, yer fulla hooey, that's just an ordinary hotel fire, we got 'em around here all the time. An' I says, no, no. Look. Just look. Ya can see the Devil in there, laughin' in the flames. He's just laughin' an' laughin'. Laughin' at Lloyd an' his wife, Lily, but especially laughin' at Lloyd's wife, Lily, fer fallin' down from Grace by sleepin' in there with that American fella, Dillinger, did the killin' up at Bienfait last week. *(beat)* So I told her that, an' then I turned around an' hightailed it back here, just like ya said to. *(beat)* Do ya think they're gonna' come?

LLOYD   Just like the prodigal son?

MURRAY   Yeah. Are we gonna' kill 'em when they do?

LLOYD   Yeah. That's right.

MURRAY   It's alright ta kill 'em, Lloyd…

LLOYD   I know.

MURRAY   It's alright ta kill 'em 'cause their souls are already in Hell.

LLOYD   That's right, Murray.

             LLOYD motions for MURRAY to lean close.
             MURRAY does.

             LLOYD grabs Murray by the neck and starts to
             strangle him.

             MURRAY grabs LLOYD by the arms and pulls
             back, lifting LLOYD out of his wheelchair. The
             men appear to be dancing as they fight. Their
             motion sets the dancehall's mirror ball spinning.

You lied to me, Murray. You lied about Lily. I hate liars. You lied about Dillinger; I hate liars, I just hate them!

LLOYD is out of control. So is MURRAY.

LLOYD	MURRAY
You liar! You liar! You lied to me; you lied to me, don't ever lie to me! I hate liars! I just hate 'em!	Lloyd! Lloyd! Stop it! Stop it! Yer goin' crazy! Stop it! Yer hurtin' me'. Stop it! I'm yer friend! Stop it, Lloyd, I'm yer friend!

MURRAY has LLOYD by the throat now, strangling him.

MURRAY takes hold of LLOYD's head with both hands and gives it a sharp twist.

He breaks LLOYD's neck.

LLOYD collapses onto MURRAY.

MURRAY slowly lowers LLOYD to the floor.

Silence.

LLOYD lies very still.

MURRAY prods him with his foot.

MURRAY   Lloyd?

Pause.

Lloyd?

Pause.

Jesus Christ, he's dead. Oh, Jesus, Jesus, Jesus. Jesus, he's dead, an' I killed him. *(beat)* Oh, shit. Oh, God. I killed him.

MURRAY bolts over to the double doors and throws them open. He is engulfed in blackness.

Chriiiiiiiiiiiiiist! *(beat)* Oh, Christ, I killed him, an' what am I gonna' do?

Pause.

MURRAY takes out his handkerchief and begins to wipe his fingerprints off anything he might have touched.

In the course of wiping his prints off things, he picks up LLOYD's unfinished bottle of whisky.

Pause.

We... we... we drank this bottle already tonight. I took it away an' filled it with gasoline just like ya said, Lloyd. What are ya doin', bringin' it back like that. What are ya doin'? *(beat)* Quit lookin' at me. Quit lookin' at me, Lloyd. I done what ya said, so you got no call lookin' at me. *(beat)* Lloyd? Lloyd?

MURRAY goes over to LLOYD and, once again, prods him with his foot.

LLOYD rolls over.

MURRAY screams and jumps away, as if he'd just stepped on a rattlesnake.

Chriiiiiiiiiiiisssssst!

He stops on contact with the floor on the other side of the dancehall.

Pause.

God loves me. *(beat)* Jesus loves me. He loves me, an'... an' He fergives me fer what I done, So you quit lookin' at me with them Devil eyes, Lloyd. You quit lookin' at me with them Devil eyes.

Pause.

The first rays of dawn, gold and lavender, begin to creep in through the window.

MURRAY gets an idea.

He slowly and deliberately goes to the wheelchair and tips it over.

Then he drags LLOYD's body over to the wheel-chair, and savagely smashes his head against the floor a couple of times Then he places LLOYD's gun beside his corpse.

It was your idea ta torch The Hiawatha, Lloyd. It was your fault. You were the one actin' vengeance, not me. I was just doin' as I was told. It was your idea, Lloyd, not mine. An' now yer reapin' what ya sowed.

Pause.

Ya tricked me, Lloyd. Ya tricked me, but now yer with the Devil, where ya belong. *(beat)* Lyin's bad, Lloyd, an' you lied. I never. I just did as I was told.

MURRAY picks up the bottle of whisky, uncorks it, takes a big pull off it, then empties the remainder over LLOYD.

Here, Lloyd, have a drink. Have a drink, you liar.

MURRAY takes a box of wooden matches from his pocket, strikes one and throws it at LLOYD.

He recoils, expecting an explosion.

The whisky fails to ignite.

MURRAY tries again.

Nothing happens.

Oh, well. You'll be burnin' soon enough.

> *He takes his hankie and wipes the bottle, then wraps it up and puts it in his jacket pocket.*

You made me take this bottle away once already tonight, Lloyd. So now I'm gonna' take it an' put it back in the Hellfire across ta The Hiawatha, so's it doesn't follow me around like a tail for the Devil ta catch hold on. *(beat)* He sure caught yours, Lloyd. He sure caught yours.

> *The front doors swing open. MURRAY turns quickly to see who is there.*

LILY   *(entering)* Lloyd! Lloyd? The hotel's on fire. Lloyd?

> Pause.

> *She sees "the accident."*

Oh, God.

> *She goes to LLOYD and tries to revive him.*

MURRAY   I... I... I... was passin' by... unh... unh... passin' by in my boat an' I, an' I, an' I... I heard a shot.

> *LILY is too concerned with LLOYD to pay MURRAY much attention.*

The... the... the bullet musta missed an'... an'... an' Lloyd musta fallen an'.... *(beat)* I was just drivin' by in my boat, goin' out swimmin', an' I heard a shot so I come in. I thought ya mighta been in trouble, or Lloyd was, was doin' somethin' crazy... yeah... people heard the two of yas hollerin' at each other all day; an' then I seen the fire an' got really scared, an' then I seen him; seen that Dillinger fella take out his gun an' take a shot at Lloyd. I musta startled him or somethin', 'cause he took off outta' here like a swallow outta' his nest, swoopin' an' divin'; an' then I seen Lloyd fall. *(beat)* I'm sorry, Miss Lily. I'm real sorry.

LILY	Quit lying, Murray.

MURRAY	I'm... I'm not lyin', Lily. I don't lie. I heard it. Seen it.

LILY can't bear to look at MURRAY.

LILY	Which way was he pointing the gun, Murray?

MURRAY	Unh... unh... towards Lloyd. *(beat)* I never killed him, Lily. I never killed nobody. *(beat)* It was an accident. I never meant to do it. *(beat)* They only hang ya if ya meant ta do it, don't they? *(beat)* I was just comin' by in my boat... comin' by ta tell Lloyd, for his own good, what people were sayin' about him... an' he lost his temper an' started chokin' me, callin' me a liar, an' I... an' I... I pushed him offa me an' he fell an' hit his head, an' musta broke his neck. *(beat)* That's not a murder' is it Lily? *(beat)* Oh, Jesus, I'm scared, Lily. I'm scared. I never meant ta do it.

LILY	*(moans)* You're gonna' hang, Murray.

MURRAY	I love ya, Lily. I do. I always loved ya. Even before ya run away from here ta be a singer. *(beat)* Come away with me. We could run away together. You an' me an' Rose.

LILY	Where we gonna' go, Murray? Saskatoon?

MURRAY	No, no. Mexico City. Just like a buncha outlaws. Or, or New York. Yeah. We could drive ta New York City. An' everything close up'll be whizzin' by so fast it's just a blur, an' the sky an' clouds'll be so big an' so far away they'll look like they're hardly movin' at all, an' we'll feel real small, like three little mice runnin' over a turtle's back.

LILY	Sure, Murray. Let's get lost.

She picks LLOYD's gun off the floor and points it at MURRAY.

How does it feel, Murray? How does it feel to know you've killed a little piece of God?

Offstage, in the shadows, ROSE starts to sing "Jesus Loves Me."

MURRAY hears her.

MURRAY Rose?! I need a witness! Angel!

LILY struggles to pull the trigger.

MURRAY cowers on the floor.

LILY can't do it; she lets the gun fall, unfired, into her lap.

Pause.

Tell ya what. Tell ya what... I'm... I'm... I'm gonna' go get the RC's. I'm gonna' go get the RCMP up in Watrous. There's been a killin' here, an' I'm gonna' go an' get The Mounties. *(beat)* Are ya comin'? I could say Rose an' me was givin' you a ride out here an' you were with us the whole time. *(beat)* Are ya comin'?

LILY I'd rather be set on fire.

MURRAY Okay. Alright. It's your life. Ya gotta' make yer own road.

LILY You're goddamned right.

Pause.

MURRAY I love you, Lily. *(beat)* We'da made a good couple, just like Adam an' Eve.

LILY Goooooooooooo!!!

MURRAY turns and flees the dancehall.

LILY cradles LLOYD.

After a moment, ROSE enters from the shadows.

ROSE   He's gone. *(beat)* He took the boat.

Pause.

ROSE moves to LILY and LLOYD. Then, with her hands, she makes a slow circle over LLOYD's corpse, gathering his soul into the palm of her hand, and then releasing it heavenward like so much dandelion down.

Then she crouches down to LILY.

ROSE   It's alright. It's alright to cry. *(beat)* We're angels.

LILY   That's right. Animal angels, crying for the stars at night.

LILY's jaw drops open in a silent scream of anguish.

A clarinet wails, high and loud, as if it is emanating from the depths of her soul.

Fade out.

The end.

An actor, director and playwright, Glen is an alumnus of The Canadian Film Centre in Toronto, and holds a Master's degree in theatre from The University of British Columbia. An eclectic artist with a wide array of tastes, his other plays are the one-act, Dada-inspired *Benny and the Furies*, a full length musical, *The Crimson Veil*, which he co-wrote with Allen Cole, and a full-length "blues riff for actors", *King of the Road*. His short film "Sparky's Shoes", produced by The Canadian Film Centre, has played at film festivals around the world. He is the first Artistic Director of The Neptune Theatre's Second Stage, Halifax, and is a former Artistic Director of 25th Street Theatre, Saskatoon. Glen lives in Toronto.